WINDOWS ON THE WORLD

SHARKS
AND OTHER MONSTERS
OF THE DEEP

Written by
Philip Steele

Illustrated by
Martin Camm

DK

DORLING KINDERSLEY

London • New York • Moscow • Sydney

A Dorling Kindersley Book

Editor Miranda Smith
Art editor Chris Scollen
Designer Margo White

Art director Roger Priddy
Editorial consultant Alwyne Wheeler
Production Controller Norina Bremner

Additional illustrations by
John Rignall, David Thelwell

Published in Great Britain by
Dorling Kindersley Limited,
9 Henrietta Street, London WC2E 8PS

Paperback edition
2 4 6 8 10 9 7 5 3 1

Copyright © 1991, 1998 Dorling Kindersley
Limited, London

Visit us on the World Wide Web at:
http://www.dk.com

A CIP catalogue record for this book is available
from the British Library.

ISBN: 0-7513-6630-7

Reproduced in Singapore by Colourscan
Printed and bound in Spain by Artes Gráficas Toledo, S.A.
D.L. TO: 36-1998

CONTENTS

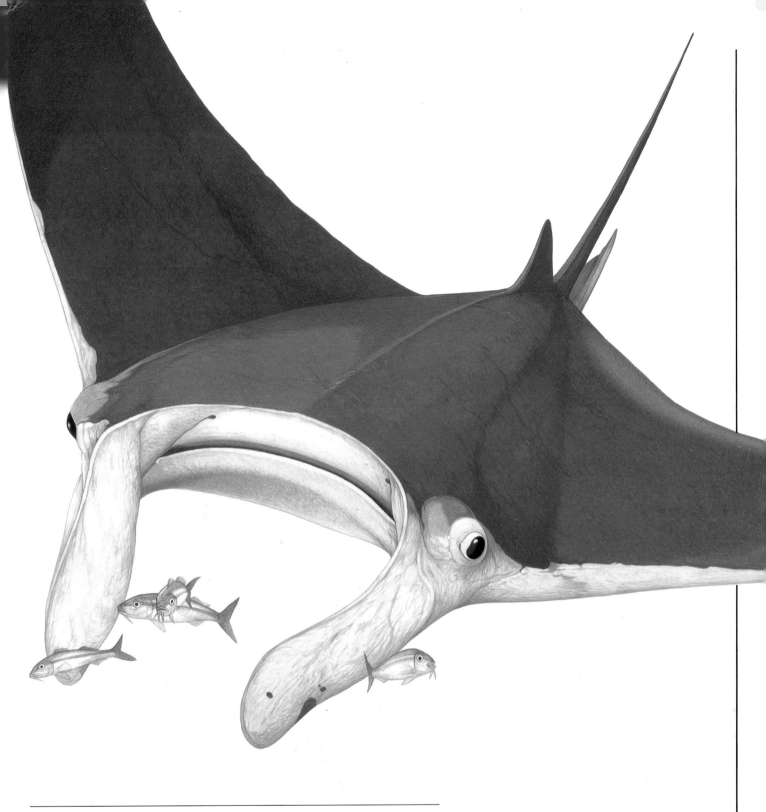

WHITE DEATH

Viewed from space, most of our planet is coloured blue, because water covers two-thirds of the Earth's surface. The Pacific Ocean is larger than all five continents put together, and in one place plunges to a depth of over 11km (7 miles). The salty seas are endlessly changing. Calm waters sparkle under hot tropical sun, while in the Arctic and Antarctic the seas are bitterly cold and often capped with a thick layer of ice.

Life on Earth began in the sea over 4,500 million years ago. Yet only in recent years have humans begun to explore the depths of the oceans. Almost every metre of dry land has been mapped and explored, but below the waves lies a world that remains largely unknown, which is home to all kinds of extraordinary creatures. There are submerged mountains and deep, dark chasms. There are strange and beautiful plants and fish that can fly. There are giant squids with huge eyes, colossal whales - and deadly, toothy sharks....

The survivor

Sharks have been swimming the world's oceans for 500 million years. Sharks terrify people, because many of them hunt large prey, and will readily attack humans. However, the Whale shark, the largest fish alive today, is harmless. It only eats plankton, tiny creatures which float in the sea. Many other sharks are too small to be dangerous to humans.

White hunter

The Great white shark is a lone hunter, and the most dangerous of all the sharks. It is a powerful fish, streamlined for speed and designed to kill. Most of its kind are found in the warm waters of the tropics, although some are found off the Californian and Australian coasts.

The jaws of the Great white are immensely powerful

Jaws

A vicious snout emerges for the waves, the curved mouth revealing a set of pointed, saw-edged teeth. Sharks have several rows of teeth, and a new sharp set moves forward to replace the old, worn set. Any victim is lacerated and immediately gulped down.

Shark skin

The Great white shark has a white belly and a blue-grey back. Most fish have scales, but shark skin is covered in minute teeth called "denticles". Brush a shark skin one way and it feels smooth. Brush it the other way, and it feels as rough as sandpaper. The skin is very tough.

The warning triangle

A shark powers its way through the water using its powerful tail fin. A triangular dorsal fin, or back fin, may sometimes be seen cutting through the surface water as a shark moves in for the kill. The fin controls steering, diving and balance.

A good appetite

A Great white may grow to much more than 6m (20ft) in length. Because of its size, the shark needs large quantities of food, and has become a very efficient hunter. Its hunting grounds are often near seal colonies and other rich sources of food.

A shark's eye view

In sunlit waters, a bather paddling on a surfboard does not look very different from a seal or sealion. Seals, squids and humans are all attacked by the Great white shark. When taking prey, the Great white's head changes shape. Its mouth moves forward and its snout moves back up and out of the way.

Just before the Great white fastens its jaws on prey, its eyes roll back in their sockets

A Great white about to take a seal

Staying afloat

Most fish have a swim bladder inside their bodies which helps them float. Sharks, however, have a very large, oily liver. This helps their buoyancy, but they keep afloat by having fixed pectoral (side) fins to give them uplift as they swim.

Swimming to stay alive

Fish breathe by taking life-giving oxygen from the water. Organs called gills pass the oxygen into the bloodstream. Most fish can pump water over their gills, but sharks need to keep swimming so that water enters the mouth and flows over the gills.

Great white shark over 6m (20ft) long

TEETH AND JAWS

Fifteen million years ago an enormous shark swam the oceans of the world. Its jaws were 2.75m (9ft) wide and gaped open to reveal teeth up to 15cm (6in) long. Today's Great white shark is descended from such monsters.

The earliest fish, like today's lampreys, had no jaws at all. Sharks developed jaws made of cartilage, or gristle, which were light, but immensely powerful. Other fish developed bony jaws and teeth. Some of these have extraordinary shapes. The sawfish, for example, has a long, flattened snout with 20 pairs of teeth sticking out sideways.

A variety of uses

Both teeth and jaws are designed to ensure that animals obtain food efficiently. They may be used for slicing, chopping, crushing, grinding or filtering. Most teeth are sharp and pointed and many have sharp serrated edges which can easily slice through tough flesh. In an attack on large prey, a shark will often clamp its teeth on the victim, shake its head from side to side and "saw off" a piece of flesh.

Megabite!

The jawbone of a shark is lined with disposable teeth. The front row is used for biting prey, while the rows behind are folded flat in the fleshy jaw. The teeth in the reserve rows move forwards to replace the teeth in the front row every 10 days or so.

Tiger shark   Great white shark   Mako shark

Jaws of a Grey shark

The gristly jaws of the Grey shark are operated by immensely powerful muscles. The upper and lower jaws bite together with great force, making it very hard for a victim to escape the slashing teeth.

The loosely attached biting teeth of the shark are often lost during fights

Tiger shark

Jaws of the Tiger shark

The snub-snouted Tiger shark has jaws with large teeth designed for cutting. Each of these razors is saw-edged, curving back to a deep notch. Tiger sharks will launch mass attacks on large prey, and many humans have fallen victim to the deadly jaws.

Crocodile victims

The Estuarine or Saltwater crocodile is the fiercest of all sea reptiles. Its long snout is lined with vicious teeth, and its jaws can crush a victim by exerting a pressure of nearly 700kg (1,543lb). This gigantic crocodile will attack people shipwrecked in coastal water, and preys on sea and land alike.

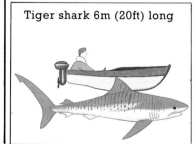

Tiger shark 6m (20ft) long

A sudden death

There are about 600 species of wrasse, ranging in size from 3m (10ft) to small fishes only 8cm (3in) long. They are found on tropical reefs. The Slingjaws are amongst the stranger species of wrasse. While many fish can move their mouth forwards to grasp prey or nibble at weeds, this wrasse can slide its whole jaw forwards when its mouth is open. This gives it a great advantage over other fish, because it can approach unsuspecting small fishes or shrimps.(1) It then shoots out its jaw, gulping them down at speed.(2)

Lemon shark

The Grey shark attacks people

Mouths like sieves

Whales which hunt seals or large squid have jaws full of teeth. Whales which eat smaller prey, such as plankton, scoop their food from the sea through plates of a fibrous material called baleen or whalebone.

The jawless lampreys

The lampreys are primitive fish with skeletons made of cartilage. They have no jaws and their mouths are round suckers which grip on to the sides of fish or whales. The suckers contain small, horny teeth which are used to rasp away at their prey.

Viperfish

Long, barbed fangs give the mouth of the viperfish a ferocious appearance. They are used to grasp small fishes and prawns. The prey is lured to its death by a light dangling above the head of the viperfish and by light organs inside the mouth.

A WORLD BENEATH THE WAVES

The seas of the world are forever in motion. They all run into one another and are affected by the spinning of the Earth. They are also subject to the pulling force, or gravity, of the Moon, and this causes the tides which make the sea level rise and fall each day. Many sea creatures have learned to live with the changing tides, and their lives revolve around the sea's ceaseless ebb and flow.

The oceans affect the weather on Earth, and are affected by it in turn. Winds and storms create swells and whip up huge waves. These crash against the shore line, making it hard for sea creatures to live in this surf, as it stirs up shingle and pebbles, and foams over jagged rocks.

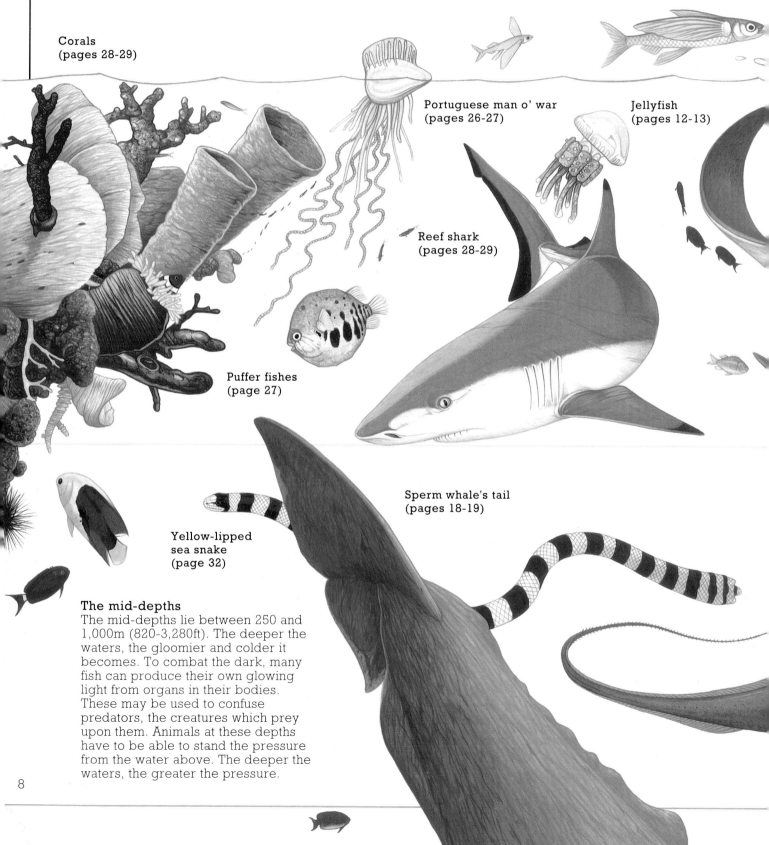

Corals
(pages 28-29)

Portuguese man o' war
(pages 26-27)

Jellyfish
(pages 12-13)

Reef shark
(pages 28-29)

Puffer fishes
(page 27)

Sperm whale's tail
(pages 18-19)

Yellow-lipped
sea snake
(page 32)

The mid-depths
The mid-depths lie between 250 and 1,000m (820-3,280ft). The deeper the waters, the gloomier and colder it becomes. To combat the dark, many fish can produce their own glowing light from organs in their bodies. These may be used to confuse predators, the creatures which prey upon them. Animals at these depths have to be able to stand the pressure from the water above. The deeper the waters, the greater the pressure.

Within the oceans, there are flowing movements called currents. These carry cold water from the polar regions or warm water from the tropics. For example, the Gulf Stream is a current which brings warm water from the Caribbean Sea towards north-western Europe. Many small creatures and plants float along with the oceans' currents.

The ocean's depths

The average depth of the sea is 3,790m (12,430ft). Coastal waters are often shallow, but the open ocean may be very deep. The sea bed, like the dry land, has very high mountains and deep gorges. One great chasm in the Pacific Ocean descends to a depth of 11,034m (36,200ft).

Flying fishes
(page 43)

Surface waters

Near the surface, the sea receives warmth and light from the Sun. Tiny plants and animals live here, and are preyed upon by other creatures. Surface-dwelling fish often have silvery undersides which makes them hard to see against the sunlight, if attacked from underneath.

Lobsters
(pages 24-25)

Manta ray
(pages 38-39)

Octopuses
(pages 20-21)

250m (820ft)

Moray eels
(page 48)

Conger eel
(pages 48-49)

Gulper eel
(page 49)

Frilled shark
(page 35)

500m (1,640ft)

Teeming with life

The sea is home to countless creatures. Over the ages many different life forms have developed, or evolved. Some live on the shoreline, whilst others survive in the open ocean. Some must come to the surface to breathe air. Others can extract life-giving oxygen from the water.

In a class of their own

How do we describe different animals? In what ways are they similar and how do they differ? Scientists divide and sub-divide the animal kingdom into groups called phyla, classes, orders, families and genera. Animals which are essentially the same are said to belong to the same species. There are many different animal groups living in the sea.

zooplankton	Floating small creatures; tiny organisms, eggs and larvae of fish and crabs	
worms	Carnivores or filter feeders, these include ribbon and round worms	
coelenterates	This group of sea creatures includes sea anemones and jellyfish	
molluscs	Shellfish, sea-slugs, squid and octopuses are all molluscs	
crustaceans	Crabs, lobsters, prawns, barnacles and copepods belong to this class	
echinoderms	Starfish, sea urchins, sea lilies and sea cucumbers are all related animals	
jawless fish	Lampreys and hagfish are primitive fish which have no jaws	
cartilaginous fish	Sharks and rays have skeletons made of gristle, not bone	
bony fish	The majority of fish - 90 per cent - have bony skeletons	
reptiles	Scaly and cold-blooded, sea snakes and saltwater crocodiles breathe air	
mammals	Warm-blooded and breathing air, whales and seals are mammals	

Squids
(pages 18-21)

The abyss

Below 4,000m (13,000ft), the depths of the ocean are called the abyss. Sea creatures of the abyss wait for scraps of food and dead animals to drift down from the upper waters. The ocean bed is often covered with oozing slime, which is a rich source of food. Food particles from shallow seas may be washed out into the deeper oceans by strong currents.

Deep waters

No daylight filters down to depths below 100m (330ft) m. This is a dark, cold world. The pressure of the water increases, and humans can only survive if they are protected by the hull of a special submarine. For fish that hunt, prey is scarce at these depths, so many deep-sea predators have huge, gaping mouths and curved teeth - nothing must escape!

Giant squid
(pages 18-19)

1,000m (3,280ft)

Deep-sea fish

Some deep-sea fish have glowing lures, which attract prey towards their open jaws. At great depths, many fish are virtually blind. To find their prey, they rely on their sense of taste or on the band of sense organs, the lateral line, which runs along their sides. Deep-sea fish move slowly, waiting for a meal to come their way.

Megamouth shark
(page 35)

Sperm whale
(pages 18-19)

2,000m (6,560ft)

Linophryne
(pages 46-47)

Thaumatichthys
(page 47)

Hatchet fish
(page 45)

Melanocoetus
(page 46)

Tripod fish
(page 45)

Gigantactis
(pages 46-47)

3,000m (9,850ft)

11

ANEMONES AND JELLYFISH

Sea anemones, corals, jellyfish and their relatives belong to a group of animals called coelenterates. Coelenterates have soft, boneless bodies and mouths surrounded by stinging tentacles. They have no brains, and most of the body is taken up by the stomach. Corals and sea anemones look like underwater plants, and most do not leave the rocks where they make their home. Many anemones are able to move small distances, sliding over the surface or pulling themselves along with their tentacles. Jellyfish swim freely, bobbing along with the currents or blown by the wind.

A fatal sting

The main part of the jellyfish body can be shaped like a saucer or a box. Tentacles hang down from this, trailing in the water. They are used to sting plankton or small fish and to carry them to the central mouth. Sometimes the jellyfish sting is so deadly that even humans can be killed.

The multi-mouth

Floating in the Indian and Pacific Oceans, the Matigias papua looks very like other jellyfish, but it has no central mouth. Instead, there are tiny openings on its dangling arms, which take in small food particles from the water.

Jellyfish that do not have a central mouth are called root-mouthed

The corals

Corals are close relatives of sea anemones. The corals also have tentacles, and soft bodies often supported by a chalky outer skeleton. When disturbed, they shrink back into this structure. Many corals live in large groups called colonies.

The Compass jellyfish stuns prey with its trailing tentacles

The Compass

The Compass jellyfish has a bell-shaped body 3cm (1in) across and can be seen in warmer waters. It has long, trailing tentacles and brown and cream stripes which radiate from the centre of its body, like the markings on the dial of an old ship's compass.

Lying in wait

The Beadlet anemone is 7cm (2.8in) high and may be seen, when the tide is low, on rocks in the North Atlantic Ocean and Mediterranean Sea. It looks like a blob of red, brown or green jelly and has an opening at the centre. Underwater, it opens out its tentacles, which are armed with stinging cells, to trap its prey. Contact with any object triggers these stinging cells, or nematocysts, into action. They inflate and release tiny, barbed threads which lashes into the prey like miniature harpoons. The stunned prey is grasped by the waving tentacles, or beats a hasty retreat.

A Shore clingfish will retreat if stung by a Beadlet anemone

Escaping danger

In tropical seas, the deadly tentacles of Stoichactis kenti, the Giant sea anemone, give shelter to the brightly-coloured Clownfish. A special coating on their bodies protects the Clownfish from the anemone's sting, and they can hide safely from their enemies.

The Common jellyfish measures about 25cm (10in) across

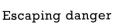

Stoichactis kenti can measure 1m (3ft) across

Tealia felina

Common jellyfish

The umbrella-shaped body of the Common jellyfish is made of transparent jelly with a bluish tinge. It is found along warmer coasts, where it feeds on tiny particles of food that it gathers from the water.

Actinia tenebrosa

CLAMS AND CLINGERS

Empty seashells are piled high on many beaches, pounded by the waves until they break up in the shingle. Many shells have a pearly sheen, colourful markings or beautiful shapes. Shells containing the living creatures may be found nearby, buried in the sand or clinging tightly to rocks and reefs.

Seashells are the hard outer casings of creatures called molluscs. This group of animals also includes the slugs and snails you find in the garden, and larger sea creatures with tentacles, such as squids and octopuses. All molluscs have soft, boneless bodies.

Conches are molluscs with single shells. Like land snails, they look as if they crawl on their bellies, and so are called gastropods, or "stomach-footed". Many molluscs, such as clams and razors, have a shell with two hinged sections. They are called bivalves.

The biggest seashell
The largest bivalve in the world is found in the Indian and Pacific Oceans. It is the Giant clam, a monster which can weigh over 300kg (660lb) and measure over 1m (3ft) across.

A filter system
The Giant clam is found in shallow waters on tropical coral reefs. It lies with its hinge resting on the bottom. It sucks in water through a pipe-like siphon, and filters it over its gills. Water is squirted out through a second siphon.

Yellow long-nose butterfly fish

Farming algae
The Giant clam filters tiny floating plants from the water. It also feeds on algae which grow on the body inside its shell. The layer of algae forms a brightly coloured rim of purple, blue or green.

Surgeon fish

The razor shell digs deep
Razor shells take their name from the old-fashioned razors known as "cut-throats". Like cut-throats, the shells are long and thin. They burrow in sand or mud, pulling themselves down with a strong "foot". When the tide comes in, the razor shell sucks in water through a short tube, and filters out particles of food. The water is then pushed out through a second tube. The smooth surface of the razor shell allows it to slide down its burrow at speed if it is attacked by hungry wading birds. The top of the burrow fills with wet sand.

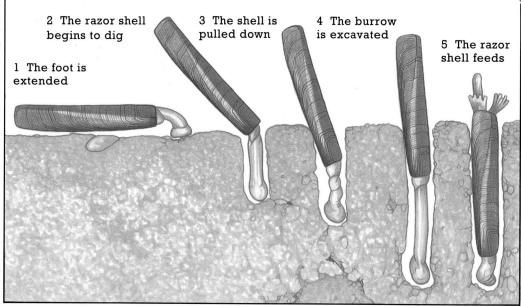

1 The foot is extended

2 The razor shell begins to dig

3 The shell is pulled down

4 The burrow is excavated

5 The razor shell feeds

Sergeant major

A mobile home
Shells often provide a home for other creatures. Acorn barnacles and sea anemones will attach themselves to the shells of whelks. Here, stalked barnacles are living on the coiled shell of what was once the rear end of a spirula, a kind of cuttlefish.

Barnacles cling to surfaces using a kind of cement

Black and yellow rock beauty

Siphon

Water passes through the Giant clam's mantle, giving it oxygen and plankton

A vice-like grip
The Giant clam has a massive double shell, and can close the two sections very tightly. Two powerful muscles keep the shell sealed. Nobody could pull the halves open with their bare hands. There are many tales of divers being trapped by Giant clams, but they are unlikely to be true. The clam does not close its shell quickly, and with its bright colours it can easily be spotted on a coral reef.

15

ARCTIC WATERS

The Earth's polar regions are rich in wildlife. The icy seas surrounding the landmass of Antarctica are home to whales, penguins, small crustaceans and fishes. The Arctic Ocean, whose permanently frozen waters cover the North Pole, is also home to countless sea creatures.

During the winter darkness, the Arctic Ocean is locked in ice and little light or heat reaches the water. Many sea animals and birds migrate south to warmer seas. During the long, light days of the Arctic summer, the ice breaks up. Plankton thrives in the newly warmed surface waters, attracting shoals of fish. These in turn attract predators - the polar bears and seals that drift on the ice floes. Whales swim north to these feeding grounds, but the feast does not last long. As winter closes in, small marine plants stop growing, and the pace of life slows down as the food sources dwindle.

The Arctic Ocean

The Arctic Ocean covers an area of 14,000,000sq.km (5,405,000sq.miles) and its deeper regions descend to over 3,500m (11,480ft). Currents carry its chilly waters south into the Pacific and Atlantic Oceans. The Arctic is fringed by icebound islands and by the long coastline of Alaska, Canada and the Soviet Union. Around these shores, the water is shallower and richer in marine life. Many Arctic fishes and mammals feed from the sea bed.

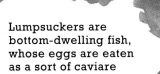

Lumpsuckers are bottom-dwelling fish, whose eggs are eaten as a sort of caviare

Greenland shark

Up to 8m (26ft) long, this cold-water shark is found in the Arctic and North Atlantic Oceans. It cruises the sea bed beneath the pack ice, at depths of up to 600m (1,970ft). A sluggish hunter, the Greenland can still catch fast-moving prey including seals, cod, squid and diving birds.

The Greenland shark has been known to attack the canoes of Arctic hunters

Polar bear

The great white bear of the Arctic is up to 2.8m (9ft) long and can weigh 700kg (1,540lb). It is a land mammal. Its white coat camouflages it against the snow and its hairy, clawed feet help it to grip the ice. However the forepaws are also partly webbed, and the Polar bear could equally be called a sea mammal. It is a powerful swimmer and spends much of its life hunting Bearded seals and other pinnipeds from ice floes.

Bearded seals

Flipper feet

Pinnipeds, or "fin-feet", are mammals with flippers for swimming, and blubbery bodies to keep them warm in cold seas. Ten species of pinnipeds live in Arctic seas, making up three groups, the walruses, the sealions and fur seals, and the true seals. The Bearded seal is a true seal, about 2.5m (8ft) long and weighing 90kg (200lb).

Sea snails

Sea snails are soft-bodied fish which feed on shrimps

Hunting in the Arctic

Plankton, molluscs and crustaceans attract many fish to Arctic waters. There are Bullheads or Sculpins, with their spiny bodies and flattened head, as well as Sea snails and Lumpsuckers - all hunted by pinnipeds such as the 1.9m (6ft) long Harp seal.

Harp seals

17

TENTACLE TERROR

Deep in the waters of the open ocean are monstrous molluscs with trailing arms, blue blood and huge eyes. Giant squids are the largest of all creatures without a backbone. Instead, their soft bodies are supported from the inside by a horny structure called a "pen". Like the octopuses and the cuttlefish, squid belong to the group of molluscs known as cephalopods. The name means "head-feet". Eight arms and two longer tentacles do indeed grow from the head, which is joined to a body shaped like a torpedo.

There are about 350 different species of squid. Most live in the open waters of the ocean, but some are to be found around the coast. All squid are hunters, eating small fish and other sea creatures. They are hunted in their turn by sharks and sealions. Many are caught for food by humans.

The monster lives!

For hundreds of years sailors brought back tales of sea monsters with long, dangerous arms. Few people believed them. Then the Giant squid was discovered. This creature may reach a length of 18m (59ft) and weigh over 250kg (550lb). The monster really existed!

A deadly battle

The only creature in the ocean depths that is likely to attack a Giant squid is the male Sperm whale. At over 18m (59ft), this is the largest of the toothed whales, and can swallow over 200kg (440lb) of prey at a gulp. Female Sperm whales will attack smaller kinds of squid, as well as different species of fish and lobsters.

Tentacles

The ends of the squid's two long tentacles are shaped like clubs. They are lined with suckers which seize the prey. The prey is passed back to the eight arms, which also have strong suckers. The prey is paralyzed and then torn apart by the squid's beak-like mouth.

Giant eyeballs

The eye of the Giant squid is the biggest that has ever existed in the world of nature. It can measure up to 40cm (16in) across and is designed rather like the eye of a mammal. Large eyes help the squid hunt in deep waters.

The diver

When the Sperm whale dives, its nasal passages fill with water. The passages are a surrounded by a waxy substance called spermaceti. By changing the temperature of the spermaceti, the whale can control its buoyancy. It can stay underwater for an hour or more at a time.

A shoal passes by

Not all squid are giants. Some are less than 15mm (under 1in) long. The fastest of the molluscs, they can reach speeds of 32kph (20mph). They swim backwards, powered by a jet of water squirted from their bodies.

Squid are often found swimming in large groups, or shoals

The Sperm whale can dive to a depth of 1,000m (3,300ft) in its search for the Giant squid

Black tang

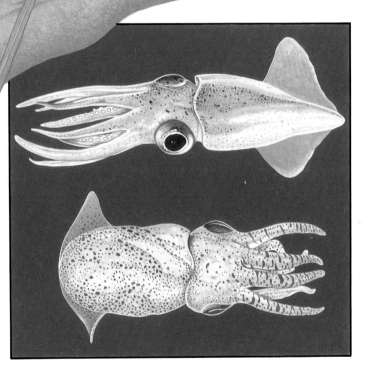

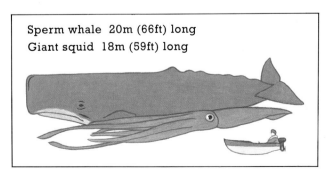

Sperm whale 20m (66ft) long
Giant squid 18m (59ft) long

A quick change

Many animals can change colour. This may act as camouflage, helping them to blend in with their background, or it may be to confuse other animals. Most animals change colour when special chemicals called hormones are released into the bloodstream. However, squids do not use hormones. Their colour cells are operated by muscles under direct control of the brain. This helps them to change colour very quickly.

19

Many-armed bandit

Octopuses lurk in nooks and crannies, and hide among seaweeds in caves and reefs. They have eight arms equipped with with suckers. These are used to catch crabs and fish, which are paralyzed with a deadly nerve poison. The arms are also used for "walking" over the sea bed.

The large eye of the nautilus focuses by moving its position, instead of changing the shape of the lens

The nautilus' giant nerve fibres pass messages to the brain

Nautiluses of the Pacific

The nautilus is a relative of the octopus, the outside of its body protected by a coiled shell. Inner gas-filled chambers in the shell keep the mollusc afloat. The outer chamber houses the soft body. The tentacles have no suckers.

Rulers of the reef

There are 150 species of octopus and many of these live in warm, tropical seas. The biggest of all are found in the north Pacific Ocean. Some have had tentacles spanning 7m (23ft) and bodies over 3.5m (11ft 6in) long. Female octopuses lay many thousands of eggs.

The Pacific octopus has powerful suckers to hold food or grapple with its enemies

The cuttlefish

Cuttlefish live in the Atlantic Ocean, the North and the Mediterranean Seas. Inside the soft body is a buoyant, chalky shield. The cuttlefish has eight arms and two long tentacles. The body is fringed with fins. For speed it squirts out jets of water as it swims.

Inside its body, the cuttlefish has a flat plate with gas-filled spaces. The cuttlefish sinks or floats in water by changing the amount of gas in the plate

A cloud of ink

Octopuses, squids and cuttlefish are all able to squirt clouds of a dark, inky liquid. They do this when they are being hunted by deadly enemies to make them confused about which shape they should follow. Chemicals in the ink may also attract the hunter and lure it away from the prey. People used to collect the dark brown liquid given out by cuttlefish and made it into inks and dyes. The colouring was called "sepia".

Cephalopods may change their body colour to add to the general confusion

Octopuses use their suckers to drag prey to their parrot-like beaks

Waiting and watching

The Common octopus is found in many parts of the world. It is usually about 30cm (12in) from arm-tip to arm-tip. Its bag-like body contains a large brain. Octopuses are the most intelligent of the molluscs. They are also cunning hunters.

The Blue-ringed octopus can grow up to 15cm (6in) from arm-tip to arm-tip

An octopus cracks open the shells of crabs by rasping at them with its rough tongue, or radula

The deadliest of all

The most venomous of all the octopuses is the small blue-ringed species of the Pacific Ocean. This is found on the Australian coast. Its bite contains a deadly poison which attacks the human nervous system. Victims have been known to die.

21

CLAWS!

One of the strangest creatures found on the shoreline and the ocean floor has eyes on stalks, runs sideways and carries two powerful pincers. There are about 4,500 species of crabs. They belong to a group of animals called crustaceans, as do shrimps and lobsters. Most crabs have a soft body protected by a hard shell, or "carapace". The biggest crab of all is the Giant spider crab of Japan whose claws may span 3.5m (11ft 6in). The smallest is the 6mm (1/3in) long Pea crab, which lives inside the shells of oysters and mussels.

True crabs have eight legs as well as pincers. They scuttle across the sea bed in search of dead creatures and other food. Some hunt live prey and others are vegetarian.

Easy prey
A Ghost crab attacks a baby turtle as it tries to make its way to the sea. Turtles lay their eggs in warm sand above the tide line. When the eggs hatch out, the babies scramble down the beach to the water. On the way, many fall victim to crabs and seabirds.

Ghost crabs
Tropical beaches are home to the Ghost crab. The crab is sandy-coloured and so well-camouflaged. Often its shadow is more easily seen than its body. It moves at speed and burrows down in the sand when danger threatens.

The hermits
True crabs grow their own hard shells. Their relatives, the Hermit crabs, are less well protected. Only the front of the body of a Hermit crab is armoured. The soft rear must be squeezed into an empty shell, perhaps a winkle's or whelk's. As the crab grows, it finds itself larger shells.

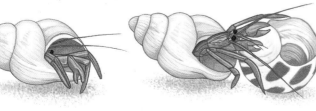

Signalling

Male Fiddler crabs have one pincer much larger than the other. The small one is used for feeding. The larger one varies in size and is used for signalling, and may be waved to attract females or frighten off other males.

Fiddler crabs are usually less than 3cm (1in) long

Soldiers of the shoreline

Great armies of Soldier crabs sometimes march across the beach as the tide goes out and sift through the grains of sand searching for food. The sand is shovelled into the mouth with the pincers. The tiny particles of food are swallowed and the sand is then made into a pellet and spat out again. When the tide comes in, the sand pellets are put to good use. The crabs burrow downwards and cover their holes with a roof of pellets.

Soldier crabs walk forwards, not sideways like other crabs

Ghost crabs are very fast runners

Growing pains

The hard casing of a crab's shell means that it cannot grow steadily like other creatures. Every so often it must moult, or shed its shell. While it is doing this, it is very vulnerable, and hides away from enemies. When the crab has moulted, it can grow in size. As it does so, its new, soft shell hardens.

Survival

Young crabs may shed a claw if seized. The limb breaks off neatly and the wound is sealed. A new limb grows and after the moult may even reach full size. The enemy may injure its prey, but the crab escapes with its life.

23

PINCER MOVEMENTS

Lobsters are among the largest crustaceans. The American or North Atlantic lobster has been known to be over 1m (3ft) long, including its pincers, and can weigh over 11kg (24lb). The biggest common or European lobsters weigh about 8kg (18lb). They are caught in large numbers for food, but most of those eaten are much smaller.

Lobsters live a long time and may survive to be 100 years old. They have ten legs, with large pincers on the front pair. They have two long feelers, or antennae, which detect vibrations and so warn them of approaching danger, and shorter whiskers which react to chemicals in the sea water. Rocky coasts provide a home for most lobsters, which can be found in depths of up to 110m (361ft). The lobsters hide away in nooks and crannies in the rocks, coming out to feed on the sea bed by night.

All is not lost
A lobster risks losing a limb during a fight, but it can protect itself by simply shedding the limb and flipping itself backwards. Lobsters must also shed their shells from time to time as they grow bigger. They hide away until the new shell has hardened, or a limb has grown to replace the one they lost.

Hunters and scavengers
Lobsters eat fish, starfish, shellfish, worms, small crabs and any food scraps or dead animals. They will also attack their own kind. The prey is torn apart by the sharp pincers and passed into the mouth by the first pair of walking legs.

Using the pincers
Look closely at the lobster's great claws, and you will see that each is different. One is saw-edged, with a scissor action for tearing and scraping the flesh of prey. The other is more like a nut-cracker, and is used for crushing shells of the crustaceans the lobster catches.

24

The long march

Some spiny lobsters make long journeys or migrations each year. Off the coast of Florida, in the United States, spiny lobsters move south when the first storms of winter arrive. They will travel 50km (31 miles) along the sea floor in long columns up to 60 strong, keeping in contact with each other by touch. They probably travel like this to protect themselves from predators and strong currents.

Distant relatives

Squat lobsters are distant relatives of true lobsters, being more like hermit crabs. They are small crustaceans with broad, flattened bodies sprouting bristles. The little Norway lobsters, sometimes called scampi, live in burrows. The name "prawn" or "shrimp" is given to many small crustaceans which are caught for food. The lobsters and their relatives all lay eggs. These hatch into larvae which float in the plankton.

Moving along

The lobster's four pairs of walking legs are used to scuttle over the seabed. Swimmerets beneath the body help with forward motion. By bending its body the lobster is able to dart backwards at speed.

Armoured bodies

The soft body of the lobster has no bones. It is supported from outside by a shell made of a tough, horny substance called chitin. The main shell is called the carapace, and the rear section, or abdomen, is made of six jointed sections.

DEADLY DEFENCE

Stings, tentacles, poison harpoons, electric shock cells - the weapons used by sea creatures are many and varied. Often the weapons are deadly. Most of them are used in self-defence, and many kill or paralyze prey. Tread on a tropical stonefish by accident, and its spines will inject you with a nerve poison that can kill you. The trailing arms of many jellyfish are used to catch small fish.

Some fish species use their bodies to make electricity. This can be used as a weapon, but it is also an aid to to the fish when it is navigating its way through the depths of the ocean. Some fish have bodies that are poisonous to others. They do not bite or sting, but should never be eaten.

Dangerous waters

Sea creatures rarely come into contact with humans, but a few of those that do are very dangerous. Cone shells are found in shallow waters and inject venom into their victims through hollow tubes that are barbed like harpoons. Some species of cone shell can cause the death of a human within four or five hours.

The Red-striped nudibranch stores stinging cells in the "cerada" on its back

Poison slugs

Many nudibranches, or sea slugs, give out poisons when they are disturbed. Some can even reuse the stinging cells of jellyfish they have eaten. Their brilliant colours are used to warn off other creatures.

Some nudibranches have white glands in their skin which give off poisonous chemicals if they are attacked

A Silverside, prey for a Portuguese man o' war

Predator eats predator

The Crown of thorns starfish is a very destructive eater of coral. The Giant triton cone shell is one of the only animals known to feed on this starfish. Once the triton has attached itself, the starfish is unlikely to escape.

Crown of thorns starfish

Porcupine fish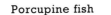

The puffers

Puffer fish are covered in spines. When they are threatened, they can blow up their bodies to twice the normal size. The Tiger puffer of Japan contains a terrible poison, and yet the fish is eaten as a dish called *fugu*. If this is not prepared very carefully, it can kill the eater!

Northern puffer fish

The Portuguese man o' war

A relative of the jellyfishes, it is equipped with half a million stingers. When its tentacles touch a fish such as a herring, a tiny, barbed thread lashes out and releases venom. There is enough poison to kill its prey, or to risk a human life.

Marbled electric ray

Electric rays

The rays are relatives of the sharks and have large, flat bodies. Some have thin, whiplash tails armed with poison spines and electric cells. Electric or torpedo rays have disc-shaped bodies, the muscles of which also contain two powerful electrical organs. These can produce a current of up to 220 volts, killing small fish and giving humans an electric shock.

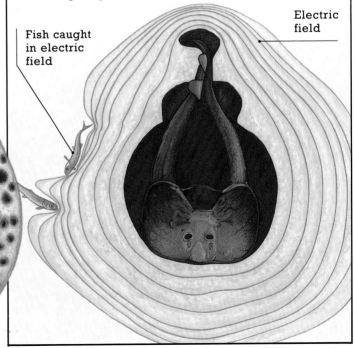

Electric field

Fish caught in electric field

KILLERS IN THE CORAL

The northeastern coast of Australia is shielded from the open waters of the Coral Sea by a 1,900km (1,188 mile) long reef. This rocky plaform is capped by the chalky "skeletons" of countless tiny creatures called polyps.

Coral polyps are tiny soft-bodied creatures which live together, forming colonies on the sea bed. Many of them build a hard, rocky framework around their bodies. The living colonies perch on top of the remains of dead ones. Over the years, these have built up into reefs and islands.

The Great Barrier Reef is the largest coral reef in the world. Over 350 coral species live there. Many build structures that look like beautifully coloured flowers, branches, fans or domes.

Crown of thorns
In spite of their chalky armour, coral polyps are unable to protect themselves against the Crown of thorns starfish. This has destroyed large areas of the Great Barrier Reef in recent years.

A crowded home
The clear, blue, tropical waters of the coral reef are teeming with life. There are scarlet sea anemones, stripey fish and long-legged shrimps. There are starfish, jellyfish and eight-armed octopuses. The Great Barrier Reef is home to over 3,000 animal species.

Clownfish

Regal tang

The deadly stonefish
The stonefish is a master of self-defence. Its back is armed with venomous spines, and its body is covered with bumps, the colours of which blend in with the reef. This camouflage hides the fish as it lies in wait for prey.

Hunter of the reefs
A Grey reef shark comes over for a closer look as it noses its way through the coral. It is found in tropical lagoons, and measures 2.5m (5ft) from the tip of its long snout to its powerful black tail fin. The Grey reef shark has been known to attack humans, but it does not do this often.

Batfish

Colourful cleaners
Markings such as spots and stripes all serve a purpose. Some hide the fish amongst seaweeds. The blue streak on the cleaner fish, a kind of wrasse, tells larger fish that it is a friend, not a foe. The cleaner fish feeds upon tiny parasites in the gills of fish such as groupers, and helps to keep them healthy.

Grasby

Sergeant major

Cleaner wrasse

Tubular sponge

Black and yellow rock beauty

Zebra pipe fish

Animals or plants?
People used to think that sponges were plants, but it is now known that they are simple animals which filter particles of food from the water. Some sponges are shaped like tubes and baskets. Others are round, branched or flat.

FISH WITHOUT JAWS

The hagfish and the lampreys are two of the most primitive groups of fishes alive today. In many ways they are like the earliest fish of prehistoric times. Their eel-like bodies are soft, and have no scales. Their skeletons are made of gristle and not bone. They do not have fins, and have no jaws.

Little is known about the history of these jawless fish. Other fish have left remains such as bones and teeth embedded in mud in the bottom of the oceans. Over millions of years the mud has hardened into rock, and the remains have left behind the marks we call fossils. However, the ancestors of today's jawless fishes have vanished without trace because they were soft and boneless.

There are 25 species of hagfish and they live in the colder seas of the world. They are slimy creatures that burrow in oozing mud. There are 30 species of lamprey, most of which live in rivers. They prey particularly on dying fish.

Vampires of the oceans

As a dying fish sinks to the bottom of the sea, the ghoulish hagfish burrow into its body, writhing in the muddy water. The sea lampreys are like vampires, gripping on to the sides of living fish and sucking their blood. They pump in juices which stop the blood clotting, and the victims will often bleed to death.

The scavengers

Hagfish will eat any food that sinks to the sea bed. Mostly they eat fish that are dead or dying. They are the scavengers of the oceans, cleaning up the ocean floor. Sometimes they kill fish themselves. They burrow into the gills of their prey, choking it with slime. They then gnaw away at the inside of the body.

Sucker head

The head of the lamprey forms a tube with a sucker at the end. In the centre is a rasping, pumping tongue, surrounded by horny teeth. The sucker is attached to the side of the prey with a powerful grip. It may also be used to hold on to stones and so help the lamprey on its journeys upstream. Like the salmon, the lamprey breeds in fresh water. It has one nostril, and seven gill openings behind each eye.

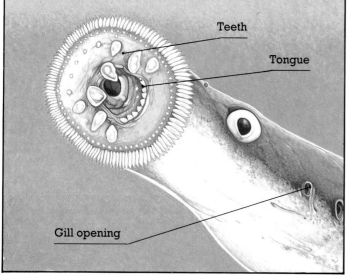

Teeth

Tongue

Gill opening

Lampreys feeding on a Sockeye salmon

The parasite

Any creature that makes use of another one to supply it with a home or food is called a parasite. Some sea creatures live all their lives inside another creature. Others, like the sea lamprey, swim freely in the water, but need to fasten upon another fish to feed. Smaller prey may die, but the larger prey, such as whales, stay alive as the lampreys hang on.

Tied up in knots

Jawless hagfish loop around themselves as they burrow into their prey. They can even tie themselves up in knots, bending the tail around the body. By wriggling, the knot is passed up the length of the body. As the head pops out, it tears away the flesh of the prey in small pieces.

1 The tail forms itself into a loop

2 The knot tightens

3 Wriggling makes the knot move up the body

4 It pulls back, the head tearing away the flesh

Finding food

Hagfish have poor sight, and can probably see little more than light and dark. They hunt by scenting the dead or dying fish that they eat. They also find food by their sense of touch. Around the mouth are four to six feelers called barbels.

Hagfish can be up to 70cm (28in) long

A hagfish starts to burrow into a conger eel

Fish can escape a lamprey by surfacing and turning, so the head of the attacker is out of the water

Greedy feeders

The sea lampreys hunt by sight, and move in on their prey at some speed. They destroy fish in very large numbers. When sea lampreys entered the Great Lakes of North America, they attacked every fish in sight. They even helped to make two species extinct - the Blackfin cisco and the Deepwater cisco.

SEA REPTILES

The tropical waters of the Pacific and Indian Ocean are home to the sea snakes. These reptiles have had to come to terms with a life in salt water instead of on dry land.

There are 53 sea snake species. Some live on reefs, while others wriggle through coastal swamps amongst the roots of mangrove trees. They mostly feed on eels and other small fish, but some live on fish eggs. The biggest sea snakes are 3m (10ft) long, but most are only half that size. Sometimes they swarm, and their bodies form matted, writhing masses which drift in creeks or float out to sea.

The eggs of many sea snakes hatch out inside their bodies, so that the young are born at sea. Other species return to the coast, and lay their eggs amongst the rocks and plants of the shoreline.

The most poisonous snake on Earth
The venom of Belcher's sea snake, which lives in the Timor Sea, is said to be 100 times more poisonous than that of any other snake. All sea snakes are venomous, but humans are rarely bitten. Sea snakes only bite in self-defence, or to paralyze their prey.

Yellow-lipped sea snake
Only the snout of this sea snake is yellow. The body, covered in smooth scales, is coloured blue-grey and banded with black. It lives in shallow waters and often spends long periods on the shore. Its poison is deadly, but only a small amount is used when biting.

Pelagic sea snake
Sea snakes have small heads, but are equipped with deadly fangs like those of the cobra. Glands pump venom to these fangs when the snake bites its prey. The Pelagic sea snake lurks in floating seaweeds and kills fish in this way and then swallows them whole.

Sea serpents
Hundreds of year ago, the sailors who explored the world's oceans brought back terrifying tales. They told of huge sea serpents which attacked ships. None of the sea snakes alive today are very large or fierce, and he sailors were probably telling tall stories. They may have seen the tentacle of a giant squid.

The Pelagic sea snake swallows a Blue-lined surgeon fish

The world's biggest reptile

The Estuarine or Saltwater crocodile is the world's biggest reptile and can measure over 8m (26ft) from its toothy snout to the tip of its powerful, armour-plated tail. This notorious man-eater is found in India, southeast Asia, Australia and some Pacific islands. It lurks in coastal mangrove swamps and creeks, where it breeds. However, it is often seen in the open sea, and has been sighted nearly 500km (312 miles) from land.

Red emperor fish

Special glands around a sea snake's tongue pass out any extra salt that builds up in its body

Hardwicke's sea snake

Fishermen curse when this sea snake swims into their nets. Although it is normally harmless, its bite could kill. The powerful body is olive-coloured, with dark markings running along the back. The male has rough, bumpy scales.

A snake's skeleton

A creature's skeleton gives us many clues about its ways of life. The long backbone of the sea snake is made up of may different sections, allowing a wriggling movement as it swims. The lack of limbs and the small skull allow the snake to squeeze into crevices and slide through tangled roots.

SHARK! SHARK!

Their jaws are lined with vicious teeth. Their streamlined bodies cut through the waves. Their appearance creates panic as bathers scramble for safety. But just how dangerous *are* sharks?

In fact, most of them are quite harmless. The humble dogfishes, often washed up on beaches, are sharks, and no one is afraid of them. There are 300 or more shark species, and yet only 27 of these pose a threat to humans. The 27 species *are* dangerous - and a few are deadly. About 50 shark attacks are reported each year, but hundreds more probably take place in remote parts of the world and are never reported. Most attacks occur in tropical waters, where shipwreck victims may well be killed. Danger zones include the coasts of North America, Japan, Australia, southern Asia and Africa.

Jaws

Like the lampreys, sharks have skeletons made of gristle instead of bone. Unlike the lampreys, sharks have jaws. The fact that the jaws are not made of bone does not mean that they are weak - just the opposite! They are designed to crush their prey with great force. The larger sharks can bend steel bars.

Catshark
This is one of the smaller sharks. The Varied catshark is only 90cm (3ft) long. It can be recognized by the blotches which mark its skin, and its black-banded neck. It is found at depths of up to 160m (528ft), where it feeds on bottom-dwelling creatures.

Blue shark
This powerful, blue-backed shark is 3.8m (12ft 6in) long and found in many parts of the world. During the summer months, some blue sharks swim long distances, from tropical waters to the coasts of Britain and north-eastern America. They hunt squid and are known to have killed people.

Thresher sharks are harmless to humans

The Thresher
The Thresher shark has a huge tail fin, and is 6m (20ft) long. It joins others of its kind to cruise the waters of the North Atlantic. They hunt by surrounding shoals of small fish and beating the water with their tails to drive the fish into each other's jaws.

The tail of the Thresher is the same length as its body

The Great hammerhead is 6m (19ft 6in) long

The Hammerhead
The strangest looking sharks of all are the hammerheads. Their heads form a broad T-shape, with an eye and nostril at each end of the top of the T. This may improve their senses of sight and smell, or help them steer through the water as they hunt.

The Frilled shark is the most primitive of the living species, and its broad-based, pointed teeth are only found in fossil sharks

Blue sharks gathered round food will often work themselves into a feeding frenzy

Frilled shark

Twenty million years ago, sharks like the Frilled shark were swimming the seas. Its 2m (6ft 6in) long body is thin, like a snake's, and the gill slits are covered by frills. The shark lives in the Atlantic, Indian and North Pacific Oceans, at depths of 200-1,000m (660-3,300ft). It feeds on small fish which it swallows whole. The female bears live young and produces 6-12 per litter.

The skin of one Whale shark was found to be 102mm (4in) thick

Shark senses

Sharks use all their senses to home in on their prey. They have a good sense of hearing. Like other fish, they also have a "lateral line", a row of sensors along their sides. With this, they can scent blood in the water from a great distance. They really only use their eyes for the final rush attack on the prey.

The Whale shark - for more about this shark, see pages 36-37

The Megamouth has a huge luminous mouth with more than 100 rows of teeth

Megamouth!

The gaping jaws of the Megamouth filter shrimps and other small creatures from the water. This shark is 4.5m (15ft) long and is very rare. The discovery of the Megamouth in 1976 was the most exciting shark find this century. Only five have ever been caught - off Hawaii, Western Australia, Japan and the coast of California.

Safe waters?

In shark-infested waters, special care must be taken to avoid attack. Bathing beaches are protected by netting, and warnings are given out when sharks are seen. Divers use special shark-repellants and work in shark-proof steel cages, although even these can be wrecked by an angry shark. Most species of shark never attack divers or swimmers. Humans treat sharks far worse than sharks treat humans. We kill them in their thousands.

Leopard shark
This shark was named after its colouring and its spots rather than because of its ferocity. It is a harmless creature which searches shallow waters for clams along the Pacific coast of North America. It can reach lengths of up to 1.8m (6ft).

Port Jackson shark
Rather larger than the Leopard shark, the Port Jackson or Horn shark also feeds on shellfish, as well as crabs and sea urchins. It lives in shallows and rocky reefs off the coast of southern Australia and is recognized by its high, curved forehead.

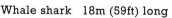

The Port Jackson shark is 1.5m (5ft) long

The Goblin shark is 3.5m (11ft 6in) long

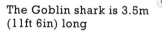

Goblin shark
The Goblin shark looks like a fairy-tale monster, with its strange, peaked forehead and downward-pointing snout. It is found at depths of about 500m (1,630ft), from Japan to the Atlantic Ocean.

Whale sharks have over 300 bands of minute teeth

Whale shark 18m (59ft) long

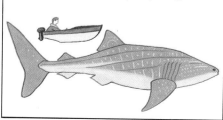

Whale shark
A gentle giant, the Whale shark is the world's biggest fish, measuring up to 18m (59ft) in length. It swims the tropical Pacific, Atlantic and Indian Oceans, where it feeds on plankton and other small creatures that drift in the ocean currents. Whale sharks often group together in shoals, and are completely harmless - unless they collide with a ship!

The Wobbegong is only dangerous to humans if it is disturbed

**Baby sharks
are born
head-first**

The egg case
of a Port
Jackson shark

A "mermaid's
purse"

The birth of a Lemon shark
Lemon sharks give birth to 10-13
live pups. A newly-born shark
pup enters the world and
immediately breaks away from
the cord that attaches it to its
mother's body. It must now fend
for itself, hunting for food and
avoiding larger sharks which
might eat it.

Shark eggs
Many sharks do not give birth to live young. Instead
they lay eggs. The egg cases of dogfish and their
larger relatives are often seen on beaches. They are
known as "mermaids' purses".
  The egg cases come in all shapes and sizes. The
Port Jackson shark has an egg case shaped like a
corkscrew. Wedged into a crack in the rocks, its
shape keeps it secure.

The Tiger
Meet a killer. The Tiger shark
is a hunter of porpoises, fish
and turtles, but can turn
savagely on swimmers. It has a
long tail fin and is up to 5.5m
(18ft) in length altogether. Its
body may have stripey
markings on it for part of its
life. Found in the Indian,
Atlantic and Pacific Oceans,
Tiger sharks often hunt in a
deadly pack.

Sawsharks
The Sawshark looks more
like a swordfish than a
shark. It lives on the
bottom of warm seas and
feeds on molluscs and
crustaceans, which it
seeks out with two thread-
like barbels. Sawsharks
are about 1m (3ft) long,
and bear live young.

**Sawsharks have
distinctive long,
toothy snouts**

The Wobbegong
The Carpet sharks of the
Pacific are masters of
camouflage. One of the
family, the Wobbegong of
Australian waters, has a flat
body 2.4m (8ft) long, with
rock-like markings. The
fronds round its mouth
conceal a snapping mouth
with rows of sharp teeth.

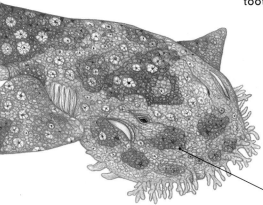

DEVIL FISH

There are over 400 species of rays, grouped together in seven families. There are stingrays, skates, sawfish, mantas, guitarfish, electric rays and eagle rays. All are cartilaginous fish, having skeletons made of gristle rather than bone, and they are relatives of the sharks. The manta rays are some of the largest and strangest-looking fish in the ocean. They have two lobe-like fins sticking forwards from the head, and these "horns" have given them the name of "devil fishes".

Rays have flattened bodies, extended by the broad, wing-like fins which fringe the body. Many live on the sea bed, where they feed on molluscs. Some species are armed with lethal weapons, such as poison spines, whiplash tails and electric shock organs.

Friendly giants

The huge manta rays are harmless to humans. They feed on small fish and plankton, which they filter from the water as they swim along. The front fins help to funnel prey towards the gaping mouth. Mantas are found in open sea, where they swim in small groups. Sometimes they float at the surface, or leap high into the air and land with a loud belly-flop.

Fish with wings

The great wings of the Pacific manta may span up to 6m (20ft). The fish is colossal, and weighs over 1,600kg (3,530lb). Other manta species are smaller - the Atlantic devil ray has a wingspan of only 1.5m (5ft).

Goat fish

Swimming like a bird

Most fish flex their backbones from side to side to power themselves through the water. Inside the flattened body of the rays, the gristly spine is very stiff. In order to swim, the rays must flap their sail-like wings, with a rippling motion passing along the fins from front to rear. The giant mantas move at considerable speed.

Whip-tails
Fish normally use their tails to help them swim. However the rays, with their strange way of swimming, have tails which are little more than threads. In the stingrays these bear barbed, venomous spines.

Many manta rays float in the water, as if they are basking

Life on the sea bed
The rays evolved their flattened bodies because most species are bottom-dwellers, hiding in the sand. Many feed upon shellfish. They find these by fanning the sand and hosing it away with water from their mouths. Because the gills are on the underside of the ray, they all have vents or spiracles on the upper side of their heads which take clean water to the gills, and must not become blocked with sand and mud.

All shapes and sizes
Rays have bodies that are flattened and rectangular, but some have rounded edged bodies. All have evolved over millions of years from a basic shark-like body shape.

Eggs and young
Many rays lay eggs that are protected by tough cases. These are anchored to rocks or seaweed, and may be found washed up on the beach. Electric rays and stingrays give birth to live young.

The wide-bodied look
The manta ray's body is shaped like a large kite. Its bulging eyes are far apart, separated by the wide mouth which stretches between the two front-projecting fins, or "horns".

Colouring
The Pacific manta ray has a bluish-grey upper side, and a white underside. Many electric rays, skates and stingrays are marked with spots, blotches or bars for camouflage.

Sometimes, it is said, manta rays give birth during their great leaps into the air

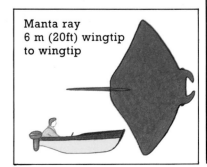

Manta ray
6 m (20ft) wingtip to wingtip

BONY FISH

Over 90 per cent of all fishes have bony skeletons and jaws. Hagfish and lampreys are jawless, and sharks and rays have skeletons made of gristle. However cod, mackerel, herrings, salmon, tuna and eels are among the 20,000 or more fish species which have proper bones. The bones give the body a strong and powerful framework. All fish swim by flexing their muscles and using their tail and fins. The fins give them the ability to steer, and a gas-filled organ called a swim-bladder provides buoyancy for most species. Most bony fish lay eggs which float freely in the sea. The tiny larvae that hatch out will often form part of the plankton that is washed along by the ocean currents.

Built for hunting

The Atlantic cod is a hunter that measures up to 1.5m (5ft) and can weigh 95kg (209lb). Its body is covered with scales, greenish-brown on the upper side and silver on the belly. Here it can be seen stripped down to its skeleton.

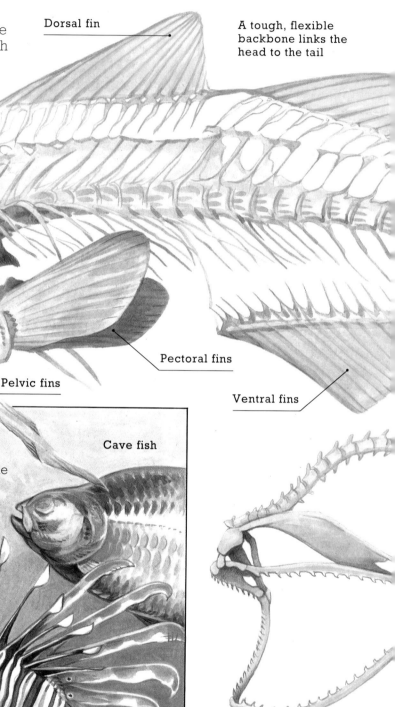

Dorsal fin

A tough, flexible backbone links the head to the tail

Pectoral fins

Pelvic fins

Ventral fins

Other bony fish

The bodies of bony fish have evolved all kinds of bizarre shapes and capabilities in the endless struggle to survive. Fins have grown to look like fronds of seaweed, acting as camouflage. Other fins have become suckers, or poison spines. Some fish have developed light-producing organs, others have feelers called barbels. Inshore fish have even had to learn how to survive on dry land when stranded on a beach.

Cave fish

Flashlight fish

Zebrafish

Gulp!

The extraordinary jaw bones of the Gulper eel ensure that no morsels escape its gaping mouth. It is known to live at depths of up to 2,800m (9,200ft), and can swallow fish that are bigger than itself.

The power of fins

The cod's most powerful fin is the caudal tail, or fin, which drives the fish forwards. Three back, or dorsal fins, and two belly, or ventral fins keep the cod vertical and help steering. The pelvic and pectoral fins control upward and downward movements. Muscles move the radial bones which in turn control fin movements. The bony rays of the fins can be fanned out or folded shut.

Bony shields

The cod's skeleton also serves to protect its soft organs. Bony plates protect the small brain and the smelling organ. Bony sockets support the eyes. The bones that protect the gills take vital oxygen from the water. Spines leading from the backbone protect the heart, liver, stomach and gut.

Dorsal fins

Caudal fin

Backbone

A flattened body

There are about 500 flatfish species including plaice, soles and flounders. They have no swim bladder, as their bodies are supported by the ocean floor and they develop flattened, well-camouflaged bodies. The larvae of flatfish are shaped like other bony fish.(1) However, as they grow, one eye moves around to the other side of the head.(2) The mouth moves from the centre of the head, normally to the same side as the eyes.(3)

A long backbone

The backbone of the Gulper eel and of other bony fish is made up of small bones called vertebrae. The eel's long backbone allows it to swim like a snake, wriggling through the water.

The jaws of a Gulper eel can be as much as 25 per cent of its body length

A living fishing line

The long, thin body of the Gulper eel looks rather like a fishing line, and that seems to be how it is used. At the end of its tail, the Gulper eel has an organ which gives out a glowing light. This shines through the darkness and lures prey towards the gaping jaws.

41

OCEAN SPEEDSTERS

Fish which hunt, or which themselves are hunted, can often swim at great speed or leap through the air. It is hard to measure the speed of fishes, but the record is probably held by a relative of the marlins, the Sailfish. Up to 6m (18ft) in length, the Sailfish may well be able to speed through tropical waters at over 100kph (60mph). It has a powerful sickle-shaped tail, a streamlined body and a long dorsal fin which rises to a crest. This "sail" can be furled during a high-speed chase. Another racer is the Bluefin. This large tuna fish can grow to a length of 4.3m (5ft) and reach speeds of 70kph (45mph) over short distances.

Marlin species

There are several marlin species found in tropical waters, including the Blue, the Black, the White and the Striped. The largest may measure over 4.5m (15ft) and weigh up to 900kg (1,980lb). Marlins put up a fierce fight when caught by fishermen.

Powering its way forward

A marlin's body is designed for speed. It can reach 80kph (50mph) while chasing prey. The marlin has a strong backbone and a sleek, muscular body. The curved tail drives it along, and the long snout and dorsal fin cut through the waves like a knife. As well as helping marlins catch their prey, high-speed swimming means they can escape from sharks.

The Swordfish

The longest snout of all, up to 1.5m (5ft) long, belongs to the Swordfish. The Swordfish is another sprinter of the open oceans, possibly travelling at speeds up to 65kph (40mph). A head-on collision with a wooden-hulled boat can cause considerable damage, as the fish can weigh over 650kg (1,432lb) and reach 5m (16ft) in length.

The Swordfish hunts squid and smaller fishes

What's in a name?

Marlins were first given their name by seafarers over 200 years ago, in the days of the tall ships. The fishes' long, beaky snouts reminded the sailors of marlinspikes. These pointed iron tools were used for splicing and binding, or "marling", ropes.

The marlin's powerful, streamlined body passes through the water like a torpedo

Bludgeoned to death
The bony upper jaw of a marlin forms a long snout which may be used to bludgeon prey to death when a shoal is attacked. Marlins, like the Sailfish, belong to the bill-fish family, named for their beak-like snouts.

As well as squid, marlin feed on smaller, fast-swimming fish including flying fish

The power of flight
Shoals of flying fish break the surface at speeds of 30kph (19mph). They then flutter their tail fins in the water at high speed, until they are skimming along the surface at 55-60kph (34-37mph). Spreading out their pectoral fins, they glide forwards. As they fall, they beat their tail fins in the water once again. A single "flight" can last 30 seconds or more and cover a distance of 400m (1,300ft), but most leaps are shorter.

Flying fish
Various species of bony fish are known as "flying" fish. They have enlarged fins which act as wings, allowing them to glide above the surface of the waves. In tropical waters the bow-wave of a ship will scatter flying fish in all directions. Some may even land on the deck.

The "flight" of flying fish evolved to help the fish escape predators

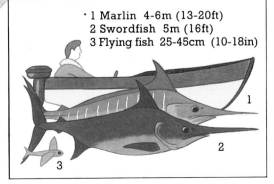

· 1 Marlin 4-6m (13-20ft)
2 Swordfish 5m (16ft)
3 Flying fish 25-45cm (10-18in)

CREATURES OF THE DEEP

Some fish of the mid-depths travel up to the surface waters each day in order to feed. Others hunt in the gloomy depths, where no daylight filters down. About 1,500 fish species can produce their own light, which is either given out by organs called photophores, or by bacteria - small organisms which live in organs in the fish's body. The eery lights often confuse predators, breaking up the outline of the fish and making it hard to see. Sometimes the lights are used as searchlights, piercing the dark as the fish searches for a meal. Light organs lure prey towards the fish's jaws, or help one fish recognize another, perhaps for mating.

Deep-sea fish are often coloured black, brown or bronze. Many look ferocious because of their gaping jaws and teeth. However, most of them are quite small.

Deadly grip

A Fangtooth grips a squirming dragonfish in its vice-like jaws 1,000m (3,289ft) beneath the surface. Both predator and prey have long teeth to ensure that the prey they are hunting does not slip away.

Dragonfishes

Dragonfishes have blunt snouts and enormous, gaping jaws bristling with teeth. There is also a powerful light organ behind the eye which helps to attract prey.

Black-scaled dragonfish

When these tropical fish hatch, the larvae grow into transparent creatures about 1.5cm (less than 1in) long, with their eyes on long stalks. The female reaches a length of 30cm (1ft). The male grows to only 5cm (2in), and dies within a couple of months.

Loosejaws

These fish take their name from their bizarre, hinged jaws which can snap shut over large prey. Most light organs produce a bluish-green glow, but those of the loosejaws give out a reddish colour. This may help them hunt prey which can only see blue light.

Fangs

The Fangtooth or Ogrefish is only 15cm (6in) long, but it has a brutal head on a barrel-shaped body. It hunts crustaceans, fish and squid at depths of 600m (1,650ft) in the Atlantic and Pacific Oceans.

Tripod fish

Tripod fishes are so called because their fins have become extended to form three "legs", like those of the tripods used by photographers. These are used to prop the fish up clear of the bottom ooze of the sea bed. There are 18 species of tripod fish. They all live in the warmer oceans, some to a depth of 300m (1,000ft), while others live at 6,000m (19,700ft). They are about 30cm (1ft) long, and coloured black or brown. Little is known about their lives.

Tripod fish eat small crustaceans which they probably detect with their bat-like fins

Lights in the dark

The long, scaly bodies of the dragonfishes are lined with light organs, which are located along the sides and the belly. Dragonfishes are found at depths of about 2,000m (6,600ft).

Dorsal fin

Back fins

Dragonfish have very streamlined bodies. The dorsal fins are sited far to the rear, near the small tail fins. These deep-water fishes are found in the tropics and also in regions with a cooler climate.

Marine hatchet fish

These small, silvery fishes with flat bodies are found down to depths of 3,500m (11,500ft), but by night rise to the surface waters to feed. They have arrays of light organs on their undersides and ugly eyes and mouths which point up towards the surface.

Viperfish

With huge fangs and jaws which gape open at more than 90 degrees, these 30cm (1ft) long fishes look more terrible than most venomous snakes. They hunt with a glowing lure which dangles from the dorsal fin, and have light organs inside the mouth.

THE ANGLERS

Various groups of fish are known as angler fishes. All angler species have one thing in common. They use a fishing rod to catch their prey - a spine, or ray of the dorsal fin is extended to form a lure. Deep-sea anglers have a glowing tip to the lure, which shines through the dark, cold waters where they live. Shallow-water anglers are often expertly camouflaged, their great toothy mouths concealed by seaweed-like fronds. Deep-sea anglers are some of the strangest looking creatures in the ocean. They have no scales. They tend to be small, but the largest reach lengths of 90cm (2ft 10in). Many species have globe-shaped bodies. These may be crammed with small fishes, shrimps, squids and worms, which are gulped in and trapped behind curving teeth.

Deep-sea cunning

Deep-sea angler fish have small eyes and some have a poor sense of smell. Their most useful sense organ is the lateral line, which runs down the sides of the body. This is sensitive to changes in water pressure. Because the angler fishes rely on trickery rather than muscle power to catch their prey, their bodies are not streamlined for speed.

The bodies of deep-sea species are normally black or brown, without scales

The longest line
Gigantactis is a slim-bodied angler that has a long, thread-like "fishing rod" attached to its snout. It lives in depths of over 1,600m (5,250ft) in the Atlantic, Pacific and Indian Oceans.

The upper jaws of the 7cm (3in) long Lasiognathus flap down over the lower jaw with the teeth pointing outwards

Linophryne

Melanocoetus is 14cm (5.5in) long, but its lure, or "illicium", is comparatively short

Gigantactis

Fishing rods
Some angler fish have long lures which are gradually pulled back towards the mouth, followed by the prey. Others have short, stubby lures. These too attract the fish, which are then swallowed whole as the angler's body lunges forwards. The "fishing rods" may also be used to help male fish recognize females of their own species.

All kinds or anglers

There are about 100 species of deep-sea angler and they are found where there is a plentiful source of food. The deepest dwelling species live in tropical waters, but some live in the icy waters of the Arctic and Antarctic. These are sometimes found in shallower waters.

The Linophryne's lure, with which it tempts prey

Spiky teeth

The angler fish below is called Thaumatichthys. It has a flattened body about 9cm (3in) long. Its small lure hangs from its upper jaw, above long, curved teeth. When prey blunders into the gaping mouth, the teeth close in behind it, like the doors of a dungeon.

Barbel chin

The female Linophryne angler fish above is about 7cm (3in) long. It can be recognized by its long barbels, or feelers, which form branched fronds resembling seaweed. The lure too is branched, and supported by a thick stalk growing from the snout.

Thaumatichthys

Hangers on

The female Edriolynchus below has two fully grown males clinging to her. The males are tiny compared to the female. They latch on to her side and become parasites, which means that her body provides them with all the nourishment they need to stay alive.

Chemicals in the female's bloodstream tell the males when to fertilize her eggs

Melanocietus

Edriolynchus

Linophryne

Fins and spines

Deep-sea anglers have dorsal and anal fins set far back on the body, near the tail. The broad pectoral fin is often set on a fleshy stump, which makes some species look even more bizarre. Some anglers have thorny spines or warts on their bodies. Their swimming is often sluggish, and some species may lie motionless on the sea bed.

47

LONG-BODIED LURKERS

Eels are fishes that look like snakes. They have long, thin bodies suitable for burrowing in mud or for hiding in crevices in rocks and reefs. The body is very flexible, and the spine may consist of up to 600 jointed bones, or vertebrae. The word "eel" is commonly used to describe the freshwater fishes which wriggle into lakes, rivers and ditches each year. In order to breed, common eels annually migrate into the open sea, where many are fished.

The name "eel" is also given to other groups of marine fish with long, thin bodies. Some of these, such as the congers and morays, are large and powerful fish with a fearsome bite. Others, such as the snipe eels, have delicate, fragile bodies. The little sand eels are not related to the true eels, but they look similar.

All in the family
The largest eel family is that of the morays, of which there are about 120 species living in tropical waters. Conger eel species can be found in cooler waters as well, along rocky coasts. Divers may come across them lurking deep inside old shipwrecks.

Snapping jaws
The conger eel has a nasty bite. The jaws are strong and densely packed, with small, pointed teeth. These are used to snap up fishes and octopuses, or to crunch up crabs and lobsters. By day, congers hunt by seizing prey which goes too near their hiding place. By night, they swim out and take flatfish from the sea bed.

Danger on the reefs
Moray eels hide in coral reefs, lungeing out from a crevice to grab their prey, which is gulped down whole. Morays vary in size from 15cm (6in) to 3m (10ft). Many species are brightly coloured, often with spots and stripes. Others are a plain brown or grey.

The European conger can grow to nearly 3m (10ft) long and weighs up to 65kg (143lbs)

The moray attacks
Many moray eels have vicious hooked fangs, while others have pointed teeth or rounded, blunt grinders. Their prey includes fish, squids, octopuses and crustaceans. Moray eels are often very aggressive, especially during the breeding season. They may attack divers if provoked.

The mobile mouth

The Gulper eel is little more than a mighty mouth attached to a flimsy, skinny body. It is a warm-water fish which is known to descend to depths of over 7,000m (22,965ft). In the inky depths, the black body of this eel, about 60cm (23in) long, is invisible. Only a glowing lure on the tail attracts the attention of other fish. No sooner have they swum over to investigate, than they disappear inside the gaping elastic jaws.

The conger eel

The European conger is a lithe fish with powerful muscles. It is often heavily built, with the dorsal fin extending the whole length of the back. The body has no scales, and may be light brown or black, with a pale belly. The American conger, found along the eastern coast of the United States, is smaller than the European.

Pollack fish

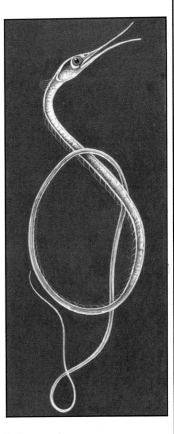

Garden eels

Like a row of plants in a flowerbed, garden eels rise from their burrows, swaying in the current. They feed upon the tiny animals of the plankton which float by. If disturbed, or scared by the shadow of a ray passing overhead, the eels slither backwards into the sand. Garden eels are related to the congers, and the 20 or so species vary in length from 50 to 90cm (20-35in).

Garden eels live in tropical waters

Snipe eels

The longest jaws of any eel belong to the deep-sea snipe eels. Their finely curved mouths look like beaks, and are lined with tiny teeth for catching shrimps and other small creatures. They can be over 1.2m (4ft) long. Snipe eels have been found at great depths.

HIDE AND SEEK

Camouflage is the art of seeing without being seen. Sea creatures conceal themselves so that they can avoid being eaten, or so that they can creep up on their prey without being detected. Many sea creatures have the same colour or markings as their background. Fish living in seaweeds may be stripy, while fish which live on the sea floor may be sand-coloured. Many surface fish are dark blue or green on top and silvery beneath. This makes it hard for them to be seen from both above and below.

The tell-tale body outline of some fish is broken up by extraordinary fins or glowing light organs, and some have bodies shaped like seaweed or rocks. Many sea creatures cover their bodies with mud or sand, while the bright colouring of some poisonous creatures warns other creatures to keep away.

The key to survival

The adaptation of sea creatures to the problems of concealment was a process that often took many millions of years. Those with a certain appearance tended to survive because they were hard to see, while those which stood out against their background were soon eaten. Survivors mated with survivors, until their camouflage was perfectly mastered.

Crafty crabs

Hermit crabs live in the empty shells of molluscs such as whelks. A sea anemone often lives on the outside of the shell and feeds on bits of food which eddy around the crab's mouth. In turn, its stinging tentacles and waving arms protect the crab.

Octopus colours

Octopuses and squid can change their colour. They have small spots called chromatophores in their skin. Muscles open these out wide, or close them up again. Chromatophores of a different colour then open out, and the body changes colour again.

Concealed shells

The shells of molluscs such as clams and scallops often become overgrown with algae and other small plants, or encrusted with barnacles. Many shells bury themselves in burrows in the mud or sand, remaining invisible to hungry shore birds.

Slugs are beautiful!

The shape of sea slugs, or nudibranches, makes them hard to see as they group together amongst the shadows and ripples. Many nudibranches have bodies covered in frills, branches or fronds which also help to conceal them from predators.

In the arms of a star

Clingfishes are small fishes of the shallows. They have strong suckers on their bellies which they use to cling to rocks and seaweed. Some tropical species have thin stripy bodies and hide among the arms of feather stars or the spines of sea urchins.

Cryptic camouflage

Camouflage which makes an animal look like something else is called "cryptic". A past master of cryptic deception is this scorpion fish. Against the rocky sea bed off Florida, in the United States, it looks just like a weed-covered boulder.

FLIPPERS AND SHELLS

Marine turtles are reptiles, sea-dwelling relatives of the land tortoises. They are found in all the world's warm oceans and many are known to migrate over long distances. Turtles are well adapted to life in the sea and are strong swimmers. They move less easily on land, but the females come ashore each year to lay their eggs on sandy beaches.

Unlike the land tortoises, marine turtles have broad flippers instead of legs. Their upper shells, or carapaces, are flattened rather than humped, and they cannot pull their heads back inside the shell like the tortoises. Turtles eat a variety of foods, including jellyfish, fish, squid, shellfish, goose barnacles, seaweeds and grasses. Some turtles are very large. Record specimens of Leatherback turtles have measured 2.7m (9ft) and weighed over 860kg (1,900lb)!

Easy victims

Marine turtles are the most harmless of all sea reptiles, and yet they have been the ones most persecuted by human beings. Marine turtles have long been hunted for food, and their eggs are also eaten. The shells have been used to make tortoiseshell ornaments and spectacle frames, or mounted as souvenirs for tourists. The survival of most marine turtle species is now under threat.

Leatherbacks have relatively weak jaws that they use like scissors

The Leatherback

The Pacific Leatherback is larger than any tortoise, turtle or terrapin. It has a total length of up to 1.8m (6ft), and a shell length of 1.5m (5ft). Also known as the Luth or Leathery turtle, this giant reptile feeds on jellyfish, and it is not harmed by their stings. The leathery shell is grooved to aid fast swimming. This is an ocean-going turtle which often ventures far into cooler waters.

The serrated edges of the teeth of the Green turtle are perfect for a diet of grasses and seaweed

Heading for the water

Marine turtles return to tropical coasts each year to lay their eggs, sometimes travelling hundreds of kilometres to the beach of their birth. The female turtles crawl out of the sea, often at night. They scoop out hollows on sandy beaches, and lay between 80 and 180 eggs in a clutch. Several clutches of eggs may be laid in one season. When the baby turtles hatch out, they have to dig their way out of the sand, before scuttling down the beach to the waterline. Many never reach the sea. They are attacked and eaten by predators such as crabs, seabirds, and lizards, as well as by stray dogs or pigs.

Turtles incubate for two to three months before they hatch out

Green turtle

Adult Green turtles are mostly vegetarians and feed on algae and turtle grass. They have been much hunted to make turtle soup. They may migrate long distances, travelling as much as 2,000km (1,250 miles). The Green turtles nest on tropical beaches around the world.

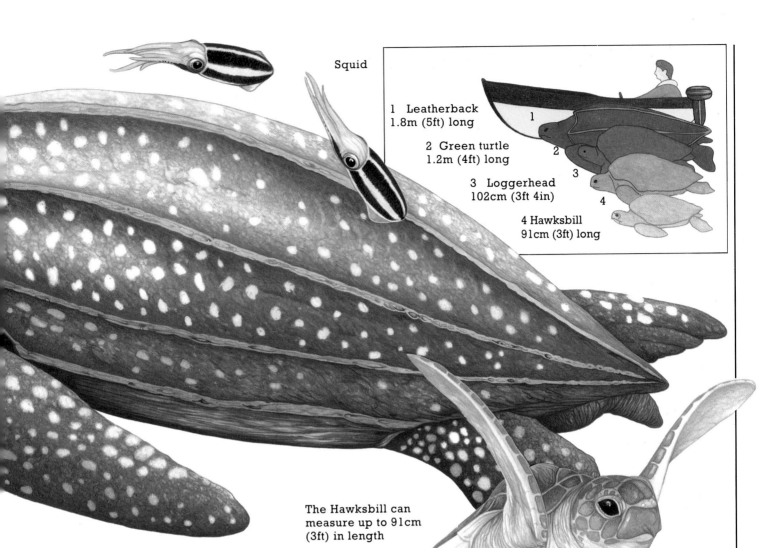

Squid

1 Leatherback
1.8m (5ft) long

2 Green turtle
1.2m (4ft) long

3 Loggerhead
102cm (3ft 4in)

4 Hawksbill
91cm (3ft) long

The Hawksbill can
measure up to 91cm
(3ft) in length

Hawksbill turtle
This marine turtle has a
beak-like snout, which it
uses to probe nooks and
crannies in coral reefs. It
feeds upon seaweeds,
corals, sponges and sea
anemones. The Hawksbill
has been hunted for its
beautifully patterned shell,
which is then made into
ornaments for sale.

The Green turtle
uses her strong hind
flippers to dig a
hole in sand before
laying her eggs

The Loggerhead
A large head is a particular feature
of this turtle. The powerful jaws can
even crush a large clam. Food
sources vary around the tropical
seas where Loggerhead turtles
live, so their diet also varies.
Some eat Horseshoe crabs,
while others catch shellfish,
sponges, prawns or fish.
There are also some
Loggerhead turtles
that eat aquatic plants
and jellyfish.

53

LEVIATHAN!

The name Leviathan is taken from the Old Testament of the Bible. It described a huge sea monster, and was later used as a name for any of the giant whales. The Blue whale or Sibbald's rorqual is the largest mammal ever known on Earth. In the southern oceans, female Blue whales average lengths of 26m (85ft) and weigh 109 tonnes. The males average 24m (79ft), with a weight of about 85 tonnes. Large specimens are increasingly rare. The largest ever recorded was over 33m (108ft) long, and the record weight stands at about 177 tonnes.

Whales are mammals, the descendants of prehistoric land creatures which probably entered the water in search of shoals of fish, and remained to live in the oceans. Whales look like huge fish, and spend all their lives in the water. However, they are still warm-blooded animals which need to breathe air. Like other mammals they give birth to live young and feed them with milk.

Blue whales
The Blue whales are found in the North Atlantic, the Pacific and the Southern oceans. They migrate to tropical waters each season. A smaller breed, or sub-species, is called the Pygmy blue whale. It lives in the Indian Ocean.

Baleen whales have a twin blowhole

Squid

Killer whale

The Killer whale is a relative of the dolphins

Whales, porpoises and dolphins belong to a group of mammals called cetaceans. Toothless cetaceans are known as baleen whales. Other cetaceans have teeth. The 9m (30ft) long Killer whale has sharp teeth, which it uses to eat fish, squid, penguins and seals. It is common in polar waters.

The mouth
In just one gulp, the Blue whale can take in 6cu.m (211cu.ft) of seawater. It sieves plankton through a series of flexible plates in the mouth. The plates are made of a horny substance called whalebone or baleen, and fringed with bristles. The plankton contains vast numbers of the small crustaceans known as krill.

Eyes
The eyes of whales are designed to operate under water and in the open air. They use their vision to locate prey and to avoid obstacles. They also use it to keep in contact with each other. Whales mostly swim in the well-lit waters near the surface, but some deep-sea divers, such as Sperm whales, venture into the murky depths.

The spout of the Blue whale can reach a height of 8m (30ft)

"There she blows"
This was often the cry of sailors as they hunted whales in the 1800s. When a whale surfaces to take a breath, only a small blow-hole behind the head need be raised above the waves. Warm breath is forced out, and forms a high, misty plume as it turns to vapour in the cold air.

Dive, dive, dive
After blowing out the warm air and taking in fresh air, the whale dives down into the ocean. Blue whales reach a depth of 450m (1,480ft), and can stay underwater for up two hours or more at a time.

Whale barnacles
(Conchoderma) are named after the creatures to which they attach themselves

Flippers
When the ancestors of the whales came to live in the sea, their fore limbs evolved into flippers, up to 3m (10ft) long. Their rear limbs disappeared almost entirely. Small bones hidden inside the Blue whale's body are the remains of hind legs, showing that whales are descended from four-legged animals.

Hitching a ride
Just as the hull of a ship collects barnacles and weeds as it sails along, so does the body of a whale. As the whale ages, barnacles and sea-lice grow on the skin, and algae may give the belly a yellowish tinge. For this reason, the Blue whale was once known as the Sulphur-bottomed whale.

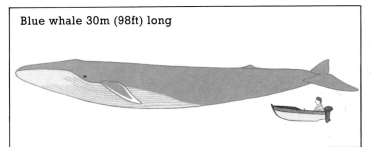
Blue whale 30m (98ft) long

Communicators of the oceans

Cetaceans are generally thought to be among the most intelligent of all sea creatures. The Sperm whale has the largest brain of any living creature, weighing up to 9kg (20lb)! Dolphins often seem to enjoy human company and show no fear of bathers or sailing boats, while those kept in captivity learn many tricks.

Cetaceans can communicate with each other to some extent, by making clicks, whistles, grunts or rumbles. They also signal to each other by slapping the water with their tails and flippers, and sometimes leaping into the air - a feat known as "breaching".

Blubber

Whales often hunt the world's coldest waters, and need to keep warm. Like walruses and seals, they are insulated from the cold by a thick layer of fat, or blubber. About 0.5m (less than 2ft) thick, the blubber lies just beneath the skin. Baby whales have little blubber, so breeding takes place in warmer waters.

A Blue whale calf nuzzles up to its mother

Whales on the move

A group of small Minke whales heads along the coast. Cetaceans often enjoy each others' company and travel in small groups. Dolphins and porpoises will often form large groups, or "schools". They may leap from the water as they travel, and ride on the waves thrown up by the bow of a ship. Minke sometimes make limited migrations, but the true long-distance travellers are the larger baleen whales. These whales travel seasonally between the cold polar regions, where they stock up on food, and the warm, tropical waters where they breed. Grey whales may migrate over distances of 20,000km (12,500 miles).

Tail power
The rear of the whale's body tapers to a tail fitted with broad, powerful vanes called flukes. The upstroke of the flukes propels the whale through the water at speeds of between 5 and 15kph (3 and 9mph).

When threatened, some whales can travel at up to 30kph (19mph)

Dolphinfish can often be seen following cetaceans

Flukes!
A Humpback whale up-ends before going into a steep dive. Its broad flukes heave above the surface. The Humpback's snout and flippers are rough and knobbly. Its flukes have a ragged rear edge and white markings on the underside. These can be used to identify individual whales.

Rorquals such as the Humpback have grooves running along their throats

Baby whales
Nearly a year after mating, the female Blue whale gives birth to its calf. The baby whale is already 7m (23ft) long and weighs about 2 tonnes. By the time it is one year old it will weigh 26 tonnes! The growth of the whale calf before and after birth is one of the fastest spurts of growth recorded in the natural world.

Suckling the young
The young calf is fed with rich milk by its mother. For rapid growth it needs to drink over 100 litres (176pt) of milk a day. The calves are nudged and touched by the adults, and herded within the group in case a pack of Killer whales threatens.

The only threat to a young Blue whale comes from Great white sharks and packs of Killer whales

A WHALE OF A TIME

There are 11 species of baleen whales, divided into three family groups. The first family, the "rorquals", includes the Blue, Fin, Sei, Bryde's, Minke and Humpback whales. The Grey whale is the only member of the second family. The third family is made up of the "right" whales, and includes the Bowhead, and the Northern, Southern and Pygmy right whales.

The chief food of these baleen whales is the pink, shrimp-like krill. In summer months the southern oceans swarm with these small crustaceans, which are plundered by all kinds of marine predators, including fish, seals, squid and penguins. Baleen whales may also suck in small crustaceans, small fish and squid. One, the Grey whale, noses around amongst the mud and sand of the sea bed, filtering out worms and molluscs as well as larger prey.

All in the family

There are 67 species of toothed whales, dolphins and porpoises. These may be grouped into several families. The Narwhal and the Beluga belong to one toothed family, as do the beaked or bottlenose whales, and the pilot or Killer whales. The smaller cetaceans are grouped into three families, the porpoises, the oceanic dolphins and the river dolphins.

Sound waves

The bottlenose

The name "bottlenose" is given to two species of toothed whale. The Northern bottlenose lives in the Arctic and North Atlantic Oceans. The Southern is found throughout the southern oceans. Toothed whales like the Bottlenoses give out a series of rapid clicks. The sound passes through the water, bouncing back from objects in its path. The echo is picked up by the ear structure in the head.

Humpback whale

The Humpback is about 13m (43ft) in length, and has long flippers. It weighs about 30 tonnes, but despite this it often leaps into the air, or breaches, causing a mighty splash. The Humpback is a baleen whale, which gulps down krill and fish. It is found in all the world's oceans.

The Narwhal is 4.5m (15ft) long and is found in the Arctic Ocean

The Beluga's chubby face looks as though it is smiling

Narwhal

Like a sea-going unicorn, the narwhal has a single, spiralled "horn". This is really an overgrown tooth and may reach a length of 2.7m (9ft). Narwhals feed upon shrimps, squids and cuttlefish, as well as fishes of the Arctic Ocean, such as halibut and cod.

Krill

Beluga

The Beluga or white whale is about the same size as its close relative, the Narwhal. It too is an Arctic whale and feeds upon fish, molluscs and worms, and often travels in very large schools. Belugas were once widely hunted throughout the cold waters of the Arctic.

The Northern bottlenose whale is larger than the Southern, with a length of nearly 10m (33ft)

The Right whale swims forward with its jaws open through the swarming krill

Right whale

The deep scoop of the Right whale's jaws, curtained with fine bristles, show it to be a plankton-feeding baleen whale. Its jaws account for one quarter of its total body length. The body is bulky and slow, with rounded flippers. It can weigh 80 tonnes and measure 17m (56ft).

The Killer whale is the largest member of the dolphin family

Killer whale

Sometimes known as the Grampus, or Orca, the Killer whale is an aggressive predator. It hunts in a pack up to 40 strong, and tears into its prey with great ferocity. Its mere presence can cause panic amongst the wildlife of the ice-floes. However the Killer whale has little opportunity for attacking humans, and strangely enough it has proved to be easily tamed in captivity.

SAVE OUR SEAS!

All life on our planet depends on air, water and light. The oceans are the great reservoirs of life on Earth. Apart from providing a home for sea creatures and plants, the oceans bring land-dwellers the rain and moisture they need to survive. And yet the oceans are being thoughtlessly plundered and poisoned by human beings. Seas are being polluted with sewage, chemicals and nuclear waste. Coasts are being developed as holiday resorts, and shells and corals sold as tourist souvenirs. Seas which once supported a rich variety of animal and plant life are now able to support little more than algae and jellyfish.

A question of survival

Fishing, whaling and hunting are threatening many sea animals. When hunters such as the Inuit people of the Arctic killed seals or whales, they only took enough to eat and left enough alive to ensure future supplies. However, humans became greedy. Today many sea creatures are threatened with extinction because of over-fishing and over-hunting.

Monk seal

The seals which live in warm seas have been affected by pollution, tourist development and hunting. The Caribbean monk seal has not been sighted since 1949 and is probably extinct. The Hawaiian or Laysan monk seal and the Mediterranean monk seal are endangered species.

Leatherback turtle

The flesh of this endangered marine giant is sometimes used to make oil or provide bait for fishing, and its eggs are taken for food. It faces other dangers too, often colliding with ships or becoming entangled in the drift nets fishermen use when they catch shark, fishes and squid.

Blue whale

In the last 70 years, the number of Blue whales in the Southern oceans has dropped from about 220,000 individuals to perhaps 12,000. In the north, the numbers have dropped from about 8,000 to only 3,000 in the same period of time.

Dugong

Horsehoe crabs

Horsehoe or King crabs are not true crabs - they are more closely related to spiders. They have changed little during 300 million years of evolution. Four species survive in the Far East and on the eastern coast of the United States, but all are at risk of extinction.

The coelacanth story

In 1938 a fish was caught by a trawler off the coast of South Africa. It was a member of the coelacanth family of fishes, which scientists knew only from fossils many millions of years old. This species was named Latimeria and was nearly 2m (6ft 6in) long with a heavy, scaly body.

Manatees and dugongs

Sailors are said to have once mistaken the group of mammals called sirenians for mermaids. Today, the Dugong of the Indian and Pacific Oceans, and the Manatees of South America, the Caribbean and West Africa are all at risk.

Right whale

The Basque people were hunting this whale in the Bay of Biscay nearly 1,000 years ago. To the whalers of the nineteenth century, this was the "right" whale to hunt, and it was killed in hundreds of thousands. However, it was protected by law from 1935 onwards.

Manatee

Dugong

Looking to the future

Humans have rightly been blamed for the pollution of the oceans and for over-fishing and hunting. However, over the ages many people have also worked hard to record and understand the natural world.

Today, the movements of endangered whales can be tracked by satellite. In 1988, the United States and the Soviet Union worked together in a bid to free Grey whales trapped in the Alaska ice. Public attitudes towards the wildlife of the oceans are changing. Maybe it is not too late to save our oceans and the magnificent creatures which inhabit them.

Drift nets

More than 1,000km (625 miles) of nylon drift net are lost by trawlers each year. Without the fishermen to control it, this netting floats away and drowns the sea creatures like dolphins, turtles and whales that get enmeshed in it.

Fur seal

Fur seals have been hunted in small numbers for thousands of years, but in the 1800s wholesale slaughter began in the North Pacific and the South Atlantic. These seals are now protected by law, but two Pacific species are still in danger - the Juan Fernandez seal of Chile, thought to be extinct until found in 1968, and the Guadalupe seal of Mexico and the United States.

Kuril seal

The Kuril Islands border the North Pacific, between Japan and the Soviet Union. They are home to the Kuril seal, a rare sub-species of the Common or Harbour seal, growing to about 1.8m (6ft) in length. This is a member of the family of earless or "true" seals. Like other members of the family, the Kuril seal is listed as vulnerable.

Anemones and urchins

Small marine animals have been put at risk by pollution, collection and destruction of habitat. The Starlet sea anemone of North America and the British Isles is vulnerable, while both the Purple urchin of the north Atlantic Ocean and the European edible sea urchin are known to be at risk.

Currents move dumped chemicals and sewage about in the sea, destroying whole food chains

The Humpback whale
Whalers hunted these fine creatures to the verge of extinction before the 1960s, as they were one of the easiest whales to hunt. Today, Humpbacks are at only five per cent of their former strength in the Southern Oceans, compared with 30 per cent in the North Pacific.

Giant clam
Over 100 species of bivalve molluscs are currently on the world danger list. Some are very rare indeed. The largest bivalve of all, the Giant clam of the Indian and Pacific Oceans is at risk from collectors.

Molluscs are filter-feeders and rely on a clean water-supply for their survival

Lobsters
The American lobster, the European lobster and the Norway lobster are all at risk from over-fishing. Lobsters today are becoming smaller in size and fewer in number.

Corals
The beautiful corals of tropical and Mediteranean reefs are in danger of dying out. They are threatened by pollution and also by collectors. The corals are sold as tourist souvenirs or made into jewellery. Many species of attractive Black coral and Precious coral have been put at risk by this unnecessary trade.

Some 6,000 Minke and Sperm whales were slaughtered in 1986, the last year in which commercial whaling was allowed

An end to whaling?
The massacre of whales by great fleets of ships reached a peak during the nineteenth century and the first half of the twentieth century. Whales were hunted for meat, blubber, oil and whalebone. They were harpooned and hauled on to huge factory ships, where they were butchered and boiled. It will take a long time for whales to recover from the long years of persecution, and some species may never do so. Some countries still continue to kill whales, pretending that their hunting expeditions are for scientific research.

INDEX